MOVING ONTO
HIGHER GROUND

Moving Onto Higher Ground

Compilation of writings by

Andrea Bowen

Library of Congress Control Number:		2021906656
ISBN:	Hardcover	978-1-6641-6622-6
	Softcover	978-1-6641-6621-9
	eBook	978-1-6641-6620-2

Rev. date: 03/31/2021

To order additional copies of this book, contact:
Xlibris
844-714-8691
www.Xlibris.com
Orders@Xlibris.com
827746

*This book is dedicated to the thousands of lives gone
too soon and families left picking up the pieces.
Thank you to all the medical professionals, front-line
workers during the COVID-19 Pandemic. You have
helped to keep us moving forward in uncertain times.
Focusing on our priorities and learning to surrender and seek the
good in all, despite the challenges, social unrest and turbulent times.
This book seeks to honor each generation and contributions that we
all have individually to make this world a better and safer place by
including excerpts from my intimate and personal journal entries.*

Behind My Mask

Behind my mask
Do you see me? Really see me?
Do you see my smile? Hesitant, yet frequently true.
Occasionally tilted when the news is not so good.
Yet I see yours, hesitant, yet frequently true.
Hopeful and scared at the same time.

Within gloves
Do you feel my hand? Really feel them?
Do you feel the squeeze? Gentle but tired.
Pulse racing with concern
Yet I feel your squeeze, gentle but tired
Grasping the only thing it can.

Dressed in medical garb
Do you recognize my body language? Really recognize?
Do you notice my shoulders shifting back, lifting my head higher
Trying to exude an air of confidence & strength
Yet I recognize yours, shoulders shifting back, lifting your head higher
Ready to take treatment or receiving the latest diagnosis.

Behind closed doors
Do you hear my pleas for more supplies?

Do you feel my helpless at watching you in pain?
Do you hear the slammed door? The bang of a kicked locker?
I hope...
I hope...
I hope...not.

I enter in with a false smile plastered behind my mask.
To render care as stoic as I know how.
While there you reach for my hands incased in gloves
And look at my face hidden by a mask
And you see me
You actually see me...
With your wise eyes...
Your eyes will not let me go before it has conveyed the message of trust.
Your grip loosens, your eyes clear and unguarded.
They too release me.
And in that release,
In that one moment
I truly see you.
Truly see you...
As your family does, as your friends do.
As my heart does.
From deep within myself
something says...
We will keep trying.
Desires just to see and just to hug my family arise
And to thank God that I have them.

A new day...
Getting dress in my medical garb I put on every day to go to work.
Does my family really grasp the tug a war in my heart and in my mind.
Should I risk it all for just one person?
I shouldn't risk it all for just one person.

I grab my mask
But...
I must risk it to save two.
Them...
And...
Me.

FOREWORD

Praise the Lord!

I am still able to write pen to paper. God has definitely blessed me since my last entry in my journal over a year ago.

- ❖ I am in good health
- ❖ I have a sound mind
- ❖ I have loved ones who care about me
- ❖ I am employed
- ❖ I cannot begin to tell you all my blessings. The highlights are:

A better understanding of my life's purpose

- ❖ Greater sense of purpose
- ❖ More maturity, development-character building
- ❖ Continued patience in all areas of my life
- ❖ Health, Strength, Family
- ❖ Strong spouse who understands and honors my life mission.

Thank you!

(March 29, 2020)

As I write this entry we are currently in the midst of going through a PANDEMIC!

I pray for protection-health for my loved ones, family, coworkers and my country. It is absolutely surreal. I pray for those who have already been affected and lost loved ones because of the Coronavirus (COVID-19). This is a serious moment in history. I give all my cares to you Lord. I write this entry while quarantined to prevent the spread of the virus. It is a time for being extremely cautious of our personal space, personal hygiene and conscious of our exposure. There has been a need to "social distance" ourselves- 6 feet away from others. Also the use of face coverings/masks to prevent the spread has been recommended. I do not leave my home without a mask or face covering. People look at me strange when I go out to do the smallest things such as shopping, walking or exercising. I consistently stay covered to prevent being exposed and fear of passing on my germs onto others. This is a very stressful time for me as I am separated extensively from family and loved ones. I have already lived an untraditional relationship with my spouse. It is even more strained now. It is difficult being away from my husband during normal circumstances, but especially now. I find that writing calms me. You know the situation is serious if I have been allowed to work from home. I thank God that I have such flexibility, particularly during such uncertain times. Our nation is going through changes in every way you can think:

- ❖ Economically-unemployment rates are astronomically high
- ❖ Socially-racial unrest throughout the country, police brutality,
- ❖ Medically-fatalities due to COVID-19 are over 185,537 –Johns Hopkins as of 6,057,520 Cases and 3,196,366 Recovered as of (8/30/2020)
- ❖ Politically-(Presidential election 2020 is November 3, 2020)

We are mandated to exercise "social distancing" when communicating in person with others. Some are not even allowed to be physically around others if they have tested positive for the COVID-19 virus. It is definitely a difficult time for everyone. Many are quarantined from loved ones to prevent infection.

I realized during this ordeal the importance of prioritizing what is important. I find myself checking on family members more, checking in with old friends and realizing that this life is precious, fragile and none is exempt from contracting the virus.

I am taking necessary precautions recommended like:

- ❖ Practicing personal hygiene-hand washing ongoing
- ❖ Wiping surfaces with disinfectant, alcohol 70% content
- ❖ Staying distant from others physically

I find ironically a new way to communicate and find new opportunities with this current situation.

- ❖ Telework
- ❖ TeleHealth
- ❖ Teleconference

Learning to work in new formats is critical to survival and to staying connected to others in work and social relations. Most importantly I have learned to lean and depend on you Lord, even more and take one day at a time. I learn to be thankful for all my blessings and count them one by one. I find myself not focusing on the petty and trivial things in life and instead embrace the things that are truly important such as God-life-family-health-my life mission.

This is a historical mile marker. I find myself intentionally doing things for others, demonstrating more kindness, patience with myself and learning to RELAX. That is a foreign word for me. I am usually busy and multi-tasking. This situation has encouraged me to see the beauty in all things and also the positive in all circumstances. I find that I need to limit the amount of time I expose myself to the news on television because it causes me to get anxious. I intentionally perform stress reducing activities like-brief walks that are functional, also writing to sort through my thoughts and try to make sense of the world. I seek more religious television programs and gospel music. I was already a big fan of this, but tend to amplify even more so during these uncertain times.

This ordeal forces me to respond in new, "out of the box ways", creative ways to sustain ourselves, economically and socially. I can't help but see how this pandemic will change our nation, individually in a more positive way. How will I respond?

- ❖ Remain open to change
- ❖ Be sensitive to the needs of others
- ❖ Be more of a guardian of resources
- ❖ Be a better steward of finances
- ❖ Be equally mindful of what I render to others, to organizations, to causes in direct relation to my goals, life mission and corporate mission
- ❖ Seek opportunities for growth
- ❖ Develop new skills
- ❖ Develop more tolerance for others
- ❖ Listen to God more intently and purposefully
- ❖ Try to better myself and community through donations, volunteerism
- ❖ Let go of past hurts
- ❖ Let go of past misunderstandings
- ❖ Be free to start a - new, fresh, clean slate
- ❖ Give others a second chance, and third chance in some instances
- ❖ Have a forgiving heart

- ❖ Set goals that impact others in my sphere of influence locally and globally
- ❖ Widen my scope-think Globally
- ❖ Be more sensitive to my physical and emotional senses
- ❖ Open my eyes
- ❖ Open my ears
- ❖ Open my mind
- ❖ Learn to touch others in new ways, instead of physically-spiritually
- ❖ Open my Heart and embrace life.
- ❖ Listen for how I need to proceed with spiritual guidance.
- ❖ Enjoy my meals, holidays, special occasions virtually with loved ones and in in creative ways via the "The Zoom-Effect"
- ❖ Remember that time is precious and we are all given a certain amount of time to spend on this earth. I need to learn to use it wisely and for the improvement of this world in some capacity and not fret on the negative and instead make positive changes for the next generation.
- ❖ Cherish the ability to see new people, places and things and travel is now considered a precious commodity. I am learning to coexist with COVID and live by FAITH and not fear.

This book is comprised of several parts. Organizational structure is below:

PART I

CAUSE: Journal Entries

April 20, 2020

Today I began a 21 day meditation offered by The National Association of Social Workers of Florida: 21 Days of Growth. Today's Phrase: Today I behold the abundance that surrounds me. Identify 50 people who have influenced me and my development. Consider why? What has changed? Why that person?

1. Mr. and Mrs. "T"-mentors
2. Angela/Robert-sibling, strength, backbone, role model
3. Priscilla-sibling, strength, backbone, role model
4. Netty/Chris-sibling, strength, backbone, role model, strong work ethic
5. My community – families along Summit Street/ E. Orange, NJ
6. Ms. Brewington-my guidance counselor and role model
7. Mrs. Sender- My 6th grade teacher/ fun educator
8. Ms. Boseman- My 3rd grade teacher and Girl Scout Leader "Brownie"
9. Ms. Wong- My 2nd grade teacher who made me feel special
10. My Sorority Sisters-strength, intellect, both inner and outer beauty
11. Handful of true friends
12. Dezi-my friend from college and artistic counterpart
13. Leanette-Dear friend and poet with such a sweet disposition
14. "Row"- Dear College Friend
15. "Bam"-Dear adventurous College Friend
16. "Tina"- Dear Canadian College Friend
17. Synthia-passion for the arts and creator of this book cover and brand for my business.

This is a task that comes naturally. I have been fortunate to be influenced by some extraordinary individuals. I have had both positive and negative interactions, but will highlight the positive: Mr. "T" took me to my first baseball game. He was instrumental with aiding me with obtaining scholarships for college. He also was instrumental in boosting my confidence and self-esteem. He and his family were accessible and helped to mold me into a very caring and dedicated woman who now reaches back to support youth in assisting them with their life journey. I am grateful for the opportunity to develop a strong bond/relationship with Mrs. "T" and Mr. "T" has now passed on several years ago.

1. My best friend – my partner for life, my hubby
2. Relatives who guided me in the right direction
3. Ms. "Vee"-Prior co- worker and source of strength during my college days
4. Prior Boss's – during my college days who inspired me
5. Work Supervisors who taught me the importance of good leadership
6. High School Friends
7. Clergy- who helped me to see the truth in myself
8. Prior roommates from college who taught me about myself
9. Childhood friends-who shared goals and life milestones
10. Collaborators- a multitude I cannot even name them all
11. Business Partners- a multitude I cannot even name them all
12. Mentors
13. Pastors both of my home church and virtually-keeping me encouraged
14. God- I am all that I am because of you
15. -50 Myriad numbers of clients and customers who have taught me how to serve with humility and respect despite my feelings on any given day.

Day 2 April 21, 2020

Chopra Creating Abundance, meditation

"Today I behold all the abundance that surrounds me."

Activity: Debts currently and in the future. (Not exactly in order of importance)

1. Financial debts
2. Self –Care upkeep
3. Transportation
4. Housing
5. Travel
6. Communication
7. Insurance
8. Food
9. Music/Hobbies/Recreation
10. Professional clothing/supplies

Future Debts;

1. Spiritual tithe
2. Housing
3. Personal Self Care and Health Maintenance
4. Hobbies
5. Financial
6. Transportation
7. Care giver Expenses
8. Additional parsonage of extended relatives
9. Business Program Maintenance

> "I create my personal abundance from an infinite source."
> Abundance means no lack in any area of my life.

Day 3: April 22, 2020

There is no amount of money that could put a price tag on self-care. "The Element of my life-Priceless," For the purpose of this daily meditation assignment I would represent my abundance pictorially as such. To pay for everything I need in the universe / my solution to pay off all the debt and expenses, is God. He is my provider from whom all blessings flow. **Please see my attached creative art to epitomize my resources from God and the pictorial interpretation of life, family, love, business and growth. Remembering to share with all and to remember we are all in this together. We are interdependent on each other for the sustainment of life and sustenance.** I am wishing prayers to all who read the words on this page. Keep the Faith. Activities that illuminate "Self-Care" are connecting with family, friends and gathers. Creative projects, sports, travel, healthy relationships, healthy partnerships, writing, publishing new material, motivational speaking engagements, physical contact, hugs, kisses, love making, nature walks, healing for family, friends, mental freedom, health, justice, relief of depression, harmony, love, self-respect, respect for all, diversity, equity, fairness, constant contact from God, spiritual awakening in all mankind –WAKE UP- Make a difference, rest, sleep, creativity, understanding, connection with loved ones, sorority sisters, family friends, family togetherness, travel, creating music together, sport together, share together, journey together and spend our lives together.

INSERT A- CHECK TO SELF (creative check from "God")

Created by Andrea Bowen, an artistic interpretation of prosperity and what it means to me (love for fellow man, health, relationships, spiritual connection to nature and God, resources that flow from God to me and my organization to those in my immediate and local sphere of influence.

Who is prosperous that I have access to: (not just financial prosperity?)

1. Parent- seasoned women- who have a great deal of mother 'wit' experience. She is in sound mind, good health and mobility to be able to support her in her 'golden years.'
2. Siblings-educated women and men, who are optimistic, strong, open to change and financially stable with a heart for the human condition.
3. Spouse, pure optimist who seeks the good in all people.

Pure Consciousness can be gaps in thoughts and give rise to anything and a need, desire without limits. Pure consciousness is useful to tapping into my inner self. Bringing awareness into everyday life through quiet moments and breathing to quiet the mind and focus on my centered thought to unlimited abundance into my life. Meditation has helped me to connect with my pure consciousness by slowing my mental pace. I usually multi-task and have my mind on many things. Meditation helps to slow me down physically and mentally, but also helps me to relax. It puts me in a mood where I am free and open to receive what the universe has to offer me. Carl Jung, psychiatrist and psychoanalyst, speaks of and coins the term, the "Collective Unconscious" as it relates as underpinning the unconscious mind, distinguishing it from the personal unconscious.

Day 5: April 24, 2020

I created my own group. Response however was minimal. I realize I must respect everyone's wishes. We are all on a different life journey.

Day 6: April 25, 2020

Centered thought of the Day

1. "Everything I desire is within me."
2. "Everything I desire is within me."
3. "Everything I desire is within me."
4. "Everything I desire is within me."
5. "Everything I desire is within me."
6. "Everything I desire is within me."
7. "Everything I desire is within me."
8. "Everything I desire is within me."
9. "Everything I desire is within me."
10. "Everything I desire is within me."

Day 7: April 26, 2020

Consider the people who stretch my consciousness, make me feel uncomfortable and have brought something meaningful to my life, uncomfortable energy.

I feel unpleasant at times with:

1. My assignments, but it reminds me to do things in order and in excellence.
2. My family often stretch my character and growth for development
3. My current life challenges of living in remote locations for extended periods of time without loved ones is a big stretch

"I utilize my conscious intentions to manifest my dreams/desires/goals."

Day 8: April 27, 2020

7 Spiritual Laws of Success to your life-Chopra
First chapter is Pure Potentiality something to consider on many levels.

Day #9: April 28, 2020

What flaws or shortcomings limit me? Name 5
1.   Personally I see myself as consistently being a giver to others
2.   Too Trusting of others at times
3.   Resources to do what I truly want to do, My PASSION on a full time basis
4.   Sensitivity to others, consideration of other's feelings at the expense of my own
5.   Not wanting to be rude-Polite to a fault
6.   Poor Diet
7.   Lack luster weight/ discipline

We flourish through giving and receiving. Nature-perfect symphony.

Circulate to get what you want is to give what you want. The more you give the more you receive.

Practice the law of giving (need not be monetary only)

Be open to receive gifts

"Today and every day I give that which I want to receive." (Thought for the day.)

Day 10: April 29, 2020

Choose 2 flaws from yesterday and establish a program.

1. Weight management that is realistic and manageable
   3 times a week Yoga-Movement
   3 times a week power walk
   3 times a week weight and cardio training

2. Diet enhancements
   Increase vegetables and fruits to 3 servings a day
   Increase water intake to at least 4 glasses a day
   Reduce salty foods
   Reduce sugar intake

3. Reduce Stress/ and management that is healthy

   Practice deep breathing, aromatherapy-smell goods, meditation, pick my battles

4. Talk more with those I love and appreciate
5. Be open to becoming more social face to face and virtually
6. Expand my opportunities for income

"Today I make good choices, great choices because they are made with full awareness."

Problem-Solving and Decision Making

1. How do I make decisions? By doing the following:
2. Remember to consider short term and long range consequences to my decisions making is important
3. Seek wise counsel
4. Trial and error is never a bad thing, just be careful do the testing on less impactful circumstances
5. How have my decisions affected my life?

Learn from other's mistakes. I don't have to subject myself to pain or hardship if someone else was fortunate to live through it.

6. Remember risk taking is allowed, but I think we sometimes want the security of a plan well developed and made
7. Remember we have to live with the decision and no one else. Contemplation and planning is vital
8. How can I create a more conscious choice?

I can become intentional and more purposeful

Day #11: April 30, 2020

"I expect and accept abundance to flow easily to me."

How hard should I work to enjoy true abundance?

There should be an effort on my part and I believe also the universe. We should not be expected to do everything. (Reciprocity)

In what areas of your life would you like more abundance?

1. Health-I would love to maintain it, sustain it
2. Family-physically enjoy the opportunity to truly live as one with my spouse/in the same household full time. Also I would love the opportunity to have regular visits with extended family free of fear of COVID-19.
3. God-closer relationship daily with him and a deeper understanding of my purpose for kingdom building.
4. Work-desire a new lease on life, new people to work with, new clients, new projects, new experiences to grow and develop
5. Relationship with self-I would love the ability to cultivate more time for self-care and introspection to create more of

an understanding for my actions, plans and goals. Also to take time to appreciate accomplishments both big and small.

<u>What changes can I release my desires into the space of universal consciousness-the source of all abundance?</u>

My changes can be spiritual. I can Pray and have actual work to seek improvements in my life. I can only change me. I must remember this. Maintain positive attitude and stand on my convictions of self-respect and respect for others always. Most of my values are derived from my parents, my mother especially. My mother's attributes are: independent, free thinker, mobile and beautiful in all aspects of the word. Her limitations are more about generational changes, as she is a product of the Baby Boomer era. What I continually learn from my mother is the importance of prayer, a strong work ethic and willingness to share my life with others as well as my ideas. What unites us is true kinship, cooking and family activities. What separates us is physical geography, distance, space, past hurts, poor choices and past traumas.

"I expect and accept abundance to flow easily to me."

Day # 12: May 1, 2020 Attention energizes-Intention transforms Law of Intent and Desire

Discuss pain /disappointment with the one you idolize, as my own personal pain disappointment would be more fitting. I have learned to remember that part of life is dealing with pain in a way that is constructive. No matter how the pain occurred (Intentionally or by happenstance), I try to remember that pain is a part of life. Sometimes it takes pain to realize your humanity. It is a reminder that I am not a machine but I have feelings, emotions and I can be vulnerable at times. There is nothing wrong with admitting my areas of sensitivity as long as I understand the importance with which I share that with. I have come to realize that everyone does not share my level of personal interest or have my best interest at heart. Deciphering who to trust becomes an art form.

Additional topic of discussion is to share dreams of /greatest desire that remains unfulfilled by the individuals I admire the most. It was very interesting to see the commonality and similarity of desires. The purpose of wanting to be loved and demonstrate love, the desire for companionship, shared purpose with another individual, human touch that is gentle, respected and desired. Accepting the personal space of another and the ability to enjoy the company of another for who they are flaws and strengths is the hallmark of existence. One of my greatest desires is to live a life that is full of peace and no hostility. The ability to accept my shortcomings and focus on creating an environment that is inviting and exudes strength and endurance to take on the world, no matter the obstacles. Most importantly, an atmosphere of love and understanding.

Day # 13 May 2, 2020: Abundance and the Law of Detachment

Today we learn to abandon a desire to get a certain result.

Abundance comes in many forms. As long as you create through desires that benefit the whole world you can get whatever you want.

Question #1: What symbols of abundance do I dream of?

Answer: Peace, family cohesion, health, strength, world peace, improved race relations in the world, equity, inclusion and acceptance. These items can improve relationships on an emotional and social level. Making money, source of steady income, entrepreneurial endeavors are equally important to me. Being able to make an impact on improving the human condition that is really what truly counts and what will have a lasting effect on society. Additionally staying connected with extended family, creating a historical impact on my culture and the passing down important life skills, values, traditions to the next generation is vital, hence one of the reasons for writing this publication, to share ideas and also to set the stage for growth and development.

Question # 2: How will such abundance affect positively on my life?

Answer: It will add harmony and enjoyment. Also a sense of purpose and fulfillment will be established allowing me to have better focus and intentionality with the resources I have. As I learn to let go of the need to be in control of my life and arrange my life, the universe brings abundance in my life.

Day #14 May 3, 2020

I have been consistent for two weeks with this 21 day meditation process. I look forward to the daily tasks and the opportunity to do some self-exploration, introspection of mind, body and spirit.

Abundance and the Law of Dharma

I reviewed Chopra Center Key to Abundance:

- Seven spiritual Laws of Success
- Law of Pure Potentiality
- Dharma Law (today)

"Do what you love, the money will be/follow" material wealth but also satisfaction, confidence, optimism, joy and abundance. I like the concept from Proverbs 18: 16 "A man's gift makes room for him, and brings him before great men." Everyone is unique so my particular gift is different from anyone else's. This gives me comfort to know that I make a difference. No matter how small the gift I have to remember to use my gift for the glory of God!

Question #1: What brings you the most joy?

Answer: I enjoy spending time doing activities that require movement such as yoga, dance, walking, spending time with family and friends.

Question #2: How do I fill this joy in my life every day in my work?

That is a challenge. I try to incorporate daily, small dosages of movement and meditation to relax and stay open to nature and God's promptings. I bring my family along in everything I do as it relates to movement and exercise to stay physically fit and overall to enjoy the company of my loved ones.

Question #3: How can you approach a life full of joy by living your life dream?

Answer: I tend to do well in groups. Finding opportunities to join others with similar interests helps. Also, staying connected to my spiritual father-God to help to make decisions that will foster positive growth and development. Continue to practice my craft and practice self-care so that I can continue to care for others.

Abundance has come to me through:

1. Phone calls from Sorority Sisters who express appreciation through word, deed and how my contributions help her to help others in the community.
2. Good weather allows me to enjoy my morning strolls. Nature has been kind to me during this entire pandemic.
3. Compliments from others particularly with my colorful and animated wraps used to stay safe during this season of COVID-19.

Viewing the butterfly video-overcoming struggle from today's meditation really sparks a sense of confirmation and peace that gifts can encourage others no matter how small. That providing encouragement in word and patience can really go a long way in helping to solve problems in a calm way and with mutual assistance from others who are sensitive to the needs of others. Consideration of others space and use of masks is another example of looking out for other's safety. However, it is critical to allow others to make their own decisions. We should not be enablers. Instead, living examples of how we can live life not necessary free of mistakes but able to learn from our choices. While at the same time being aware that we can learn from others' struggles, but realize we all have our own personal challenges that we often need to endure and while others can assist, they may not be able to remove the hurdle, but can help to make the climb more manageable.

The use of technology has been a huge way to deal with the struggling isolation due to social distancing. Use of Zoom and other platforms have been tremendously helpful and closing the gap of isolation. Respectful to those who are willing to join me in this 21 Day Meditation and those who were not as receptive was an important lesson to learn. Everyone is on a different path to how they adjust to this pandemic and also understanding that everyone has a choice is critical to learn.

Day #15 Task: Write a letter of gratitude and recognition to a person who you think hurt you at some point in life. Write a letter to only one person.

I choose to focus on safe spaces/environments and the power of forgiveness and less about the person(s) who have harmed me in this particular exercise. I have a lot of practice. Through the years I have examined my personal life as a child and now as a middle aged woman. I have grown into a strong, faithful and giving woman due in part because of my own lack of resources. I have learned to rely on my spiritual father to guide me through difficult times and the support of people who wanted the best for me. The things that I am grateful for are my treasures: family, friends, associates and mentors who have helped to guide me. I truly am grateful for the gift to seek connections in creative ways- The arts such as dance, drama and creative writing. Most importantly I am grateful for the ability to discern and decipher safe vs. unsafe environments. My ability to be very sensitive at times gives me an edge to understanding the soul of the human spirit and work in a field that relies on human connection.

Day# 16 Task: Make a list of the things that I wanted to do, but postponed, (Maybe because of other priorities or fear of hurting someone or fear of failure). Regardless of the reason, these are things that you still plan on doing.

Forgive myself in the process.

1. I, Andrea Bowen, forgive myself for decisions regarding moving to new and unknown territories for personal growth and development despite the risk.
2. I, Andrea Bowen, forgive myself for sometimes placing value on work over family
3. I, Andrea Bowen forgive myself for wanting to be perfect
4. I, Andrea Bowen forgive myself for having high expectations and expecting others to measure up to my standards
5. I, Andrea Bowen, forgive myself for not relaxing enough and looking at others as if they should do the same thing and be a Type A personality
6. I, Andrea Bowen, forgive myself for second guessing myself and not trusting my gut instinct at times.
7. I, Andrea Bowen, forgive myself for not cultivating my gifts earlier in my life.

Everything I want without limitations include:

1. Peace-Home environment, work environment and everywhere I go
2. Living in Harmony with my Family and loved ones

3. A work environment that respects my contributions
4. Acceptance of change
5. Continued quality of life for my senior family members
6. Restored years for those loved ones who have been absent in my life due to no fault of my own.
7. Good sound health for myself and loved ones
8. More time….. to relax and enjoy nature, extended family
9. Financial stability
10. Abundance in all areas of my life.
11. Improved nutrition-balanced meals/snacks

Today I remember to be grateful for everything

Day # 17: Task is to create a list of all the important things you have. Material, spiritual, emotional, etc. are included. There are no high or low limits in the things you can write down. Recognize everything you have that matters to you.

1. Health-primarily to accept and serve others
2. Strength-to do God's Will in the world
3. Family –to enjoy and learn about myself and them
4. Marriage-to remind me of commitment
5. Husband –to remind me I am not a lone and have someone on my team
6. Faith-to remind me that I can do all things through God
7. Hope-for a better tomorrow
8. Peace-to practice it everyday
9. Patience-to remind me to exercise it everyday
10. Life-to uplift it as a gift and remind me to use it to help others and not just for my own pleasure
11. Home-to appreciate my solitude, safety and sanctuary
12. God – to remember He is always with me at all times because He lives inside of me

Question # 1 how do you feel when you wake up every morning?

I feel thankful, rested (most of the time) and ready to see what the day will bring and what I need to do to contribute to the world.

Question #2 how much would your life improve if you lived with a light and carefree heart?

I would see transformations in every area of my life, family, work, recreationally, socially and spiritually.

Question # 3 how can you switch your mind to spread the love and joy that you feel in your heart right now, despite life's challenges?

A positive atmosphere is like a breath of fresh air. I can spend time with optimistic people, focus on self-care. Although that may seem selfish, it will allow me to get the best out of life by demonstrating love for self like setting boundaries, eating healthy, performing behavior that will add to my life in a productive and healthy way. (Exercise, diet, stress free activities, enjoying nature, long walks, opening my heart to receive love and not always give love. Reciprocity is important. Learning to be considerate of others is important. Also, having an open mind and looking at circumstances from a variety of perspectives. Learning to practice calmness is important to handle circumstances with objectivity, care and concern. Learning to put domineering tactics aside can be so vital to understanding others and decreasing defensiveness in our relationships with others in all walks of life.

Question # 4 how can we live carefree of judgment and anxiety focusing on joy of the present moment

I often start the day with reconciling my mind and heart first. Is there someone I need to follow up with, do I need to apologize for an action made previously? Or do I need to meditate to clear my mind and garner energy in preparation for what the day will bring? Focusing on the present moment is so difficult for me to do, I am always planning. I am learning to meditate to focus on my body, slow my breathing, clear my thoughts and release any negative energy. I have recently begun yoga. This helps me to stretch my mind, body and also connect with my core center emotionally. I conduct an ongoing Noon Day Stretch session with the people I love and care about for motivation and invigoration. Thank you "Zoom" for helping to make this possible.

Day # 18 Task Write a letter to your country of origin

Phrase of the day: I celebrate my unity with all life knowing we are all one.

Message of the day: Live in unity.

Question # 1: How would I define unity?

I believe coming together in like mindedness and accepting other's differences and various perspectives in a respectful manner is critical. I also believe unity is a combined effort to merge ideas and customs in ways that transform and create new ideas or ways of doing things; ways of interacting and communicating with our fellow man irrespective to nationality, ethnicity or age. I see it as a coming together to create a masterpiece of new opportunities. I also see unity as a form of strength or cohesion that cannot be broken.

Question # 2: What do you think of diversity?

I see a mosaic of colors. I see uniqueness of each person's physical traits, talents, gifts and personalities. I see everyone using their individual special qualities for the common good of all. No one is any better than anyone else, in my opinion. We all bring something beautiful to this world.

Question # 3: How did meditation help you realize the idea of living in unity?

The body is amazing. Often we need to take care of our body so that it will take care of us. Remember that adage? Quietness and calmness is essential to shut down and rejuvenate. We need time for rest, to prepare us for the next journey and challenge. Bishop Dale Bronner has a sermon titled "**Ordered Chaos**". I would encourage you to secure and listen to it. In that particular message the Pastor of "Word of Faith: Family Worship Cathedral Austell, GA. 212 Riverside PKWY. Bishop Dale Bronner speaks of rest as a part of restoration. We need not plateau but rest, before going to the next level in our life.

www.woffamily.org

Letter to Africa and the Caribbean's, my native land

Dear Motherland.

This is your daughter, Andrea Bowen. I have been transformed into many cultures. My name is a combination of French, Irish and Spanish derivatives. There is a lot in a name. It tells a story without saying a word. I have been transported to a new continent, America. As you well know, many of our descendants have been captured unwillingly beyond their control by savages who chose to uproot us from all we know. (our native family, our first language, native land and indigenous food-stripped only to be forced into servitude and assimilation to the Western world). I have longed to-know my complete genealogy on a personal level. I have a deep desire to know what my forefathers and mothers looked like and how they behaved and dressed. Do I have in my DNA resemblances to you? My desire is to reconcile my questions of and feeling of being forced to learn new cultures and new religious practices. I am a new breed, a mixture of African, American (Latin) and most definitely Native American.

I hold within my spirit the power of skills and talents that only can be traced back to my homeland. While I have learned to adapt and assimilate, I often think about what my life would be like if I stayed in my natural habitat of the Motherland. I have learned survival and tenacity and to cultivate inner power by reflecting on my ancestors who have walked this earth before me, whether the continents of the Americas North and South, Africa, Asian, Europe or wherever. I have learned to embrace who I am (rich mixture of cultures/ a hybrid/ a mosaic).

I have learned to embrace who I am and operate on the present moment and bloom where I am planted... and understand what under girts me. I am a culmination of richness of people who are

-STRONG
-INTELLIGIENT
-RESORCEFUL
-SPIRITUAL
-ARTISTIC

I thank my God for life and embrace all aspects of my multi-culture and hold my head up with admiration of which I represent- the Human Race.

Day # 19: Parable: This too shall pass

This was a very fitting anecdote as I find myself in a precarious situation. How do I cope with injustices I see in the work environment, community at large? There are many things I could include as my journey has been filled with disappointments, unfair and mistreatment that dates back to slavery. I choose to focus on how to break barriers, how to do extraordinary things for my neighborhood and fellow man. However, while still being cognizant of the disparities and inequities in justice, health care and within the workforce we historically have endured on many levels. My question is when will the struggle be over? We need struggle to stay strong and to stay humble, but sometimes it becomes a matter of how much Lord will you put on me and my people? How do we keep fighting while many of our icons such as Dr. Martin Luther King and Malcolm X and other great Civil Rights activists have passed on? Who will rise up? We all must, in our own individual way I believe. This can be attained through whatever sphere of influence you may have. Where do you have the most impact? What group of individuals will listen to you? How do we maintain dignity and self-respect when there is injustice all around, senseless murders and assaults present? How do we heal the 200 plus years of oppression as a group of people and also as an individual? How do we root out hate in all areas, not just police brutality?

Day # 20: Review previous tasks highlighted in my journal as areas of focus.

- I shared the parable with family and friends. The story had to do with the struggle that a butterfly goes through to be released from its cocoon and emerge being able to soar and fly high because of the struggle exercising its muscle in its wings to fly. It felt good sharing thoughts of hope and inspiration. The idea that we will evolve into new situations brings me some solace/comfort.

Phrase of the day: "Live in the fat of the land"

"Luxury" is adding to my life something much more significant than just necessity.

Question # 1: How is luxury manifested in your life, tangibly, with material goods, resources and through the kindness of others?

Family activities and gatherings is definitely a luxury. For example, I am physically living in a geographically different area from loved ones. Time spent face to face and time spent talking to loved ones is definitely a luxury for me.

Question # 2: What luxury gifts do you present for yourself?

- Music
- Dance
- Creative Crafts and ideas

- Self-Care (pedicure, manicure, new hair- do)
- Baths/soaking my feet
- Dinner Dish that I love
- Favorite restaurant
- Outings with Nature (beach/gardening, witness sunrise, sunset, astrology)
- Trips to relax/cruise

Question #3: How can you bring luxury to others?

Perhaps small thoughtful gifts, greeting cards,
Carve out quality time together
Listening to others actively
A phone call
Acts of service help with chores or assignments
Collaborating on projects, sharing the work load

"Today I treat myself to moments of luxury"

- Exercise/ Walks/ Yoga/ Stretches
- Self Care-Water
- Cleansing of toxic environments and people internally and externally
- 10 minutes of nothing but silence

Day # 21

7 Switches of happiness

- Give to your Neighbor
- Transmit love and light
- Let go of things that do not serve you
- Indulge (live life to the fullest)
- Give Thanks (Gratitude can be contagious)

- You in your authentic and healthy self is the best present to others
- Forgive

How you serve your time, with whom you spend it and how you feel at every moment determines your life.

Key Take-Away

(Awareness, gratitude and recognition of value and abundance)

A very fulfilling 21 days. Thank you NASW-FLORIDA for a very thought provoking activity. I am glad I participated. It was very introspective and helped me to calm my mind and body. In spite of the current circumstances, planting seeds of goodness is critical in developing my abundance.

Every moment of every day, I live my life abundantly!

PART II

CREATIVITY

What I have learned through
Activities of COVID-19 Pandemic

All of us are individuals and reacts to threats differently. During this unusual circumstance of social distance, constant concern for the welfare of others and personal preservation, I have made a note to self. COVID-19 teaches me the following

1. I have life-cherish it
2. Circumstances can change quickly
3. Everyone may see things differently
4. Everyone is affected differently
5. Kindness is a rarity
6. Understanding others can be battling challenges, along with me
7. Crisis brings opportunity
8. Crisis often reveals our true selves
9. Crisis can often help to discover new talents
10. Cooperation and community is essential
11. Relinquish control
12. No good deed goes undone
13. Everyone is not always on the same page as me
14. There are selfish people in this world –don't be one of them
15. There are good people in this world
16. There are evil people in this world
17. I need to quickly discern the difference
18. The importance of staying focused is critical
19. The need to stay emotionally connected to others
20. The need to stay connected to nature and the cycle of life
21. The need to stay connected with my faith
22. The need to stay active in my thoughts
23. The value in exercise
24. The necessity of prayer
25. The constant hope for change
26. The fervent prayer for health
27. The need to be loved
28. The need to love others in word, deed and action
29. The importance of being appreciated

30. The need to be respected
31. The importance of self-talk
32. The importance of listening to God
33. Waiting to hear from God through other people, children and nature
34. The value of human existence
35. Do not allow other's criticism or judgment to create my reality
36. Personal strength relies on personal self-worth.
37. It is not what people call me, but what I answer to- trash the labels
38. Guard my mouth and tongue
39. Guard my heart
40. Guard my eyes
41. Guard my ears
42. Speak Truth
43. Demonstrate love
44. Plan for the future
45. Live for the moment
46. Enjoy each moment
47. Appreciate my weaknesses/limitations
48. Learn from my mistakes
49. Remember time is precious
50. Spend energy on people, activities that can change the world
51. Invest in people, especially youth
52. Do not live in the past but learn from the past
53. Remember the next generation, they will replace me
54. Make things better for society
55. Be a part of the solution
56. Be a leader
57. Remember sometime I also will need to follow
58. Love myself
59. Take care of myself (mind/body & spirit)
60. Rest often
61. Eat healthy foods

62. Splurge every once in a while on myself
63. Treat myself
64. Look inward for strength
65. Accept that not everyone will like me, their loss
66. Take time to do nothing-but ponder
67. Recharge myself daily
68. Remember God loves Me
69. Remain hopeful for change
70. Remember I will never please everyone
71. Listen to my elders
72. Seek guidance from elders
73. Remember Rome was not built in a day-pace myself
74. Take small steps towards change
75. Entertain my inner child often
76. Remember Everyone has lost something special or someone special
77. Appreciate the small things in life
78. Ask God to open my eyes to see what I need to see
79. Ask God to help me to accomplish what I need to do and learn
80. Fun is relative and should be a part of our daily life
81. Sharing and caring is crucial during crisis
82. Silence can soothe many pains and hurts
83. Endurance is something I seek more of
84. Strength is something I pray more for
85. Perseverance is perfected in waiting and living to be the best we can
86. A mask can protect
87. A mask can send a message of care
88. A mask can hide hurt
89. A mask can hide pain
90. A mask can make someone feel uncomfortable
91. A mask can be political
92. A mask can bring joy
93. A mask can cover a many pains

94. A mask can be mandated
95. A mask can heal
96. Leadership is developed
97. Good Leadership cares
98. Love endures
99. Reading is fundamental
100. It's okay to not be okay/ not understood
101. Be ready to move forward / give back
102. Be able to forgive myself
103. Be able to forgive others
104. Do not be afraid to start a new
105. Do my research on things that interest me
106. Be an explorer
107. Be open-minded
108. Be respectful at all times
109. Take criticism with grace
110. Stand up for my beliefs
111. Pool together with like-minded individuals
112. Embrace diversity in others
113. Embrace change
114. Accept and take ownership of my feelings and my behavior
115. Learn to give myself time to collect my thoughts
116. Learn to listen to others
117. Be sensitive to the needs of others
118. Never allow anyone to bully me. Stand for something or fall for anything
119. Respect other's choices, even if it is not in alignment with mine
120. Keep my enemies within my circle of prayers
121. Pray for those who demonstrate hate towards me or my kinship
122. Pray for healing of the world and myself
123. Ask God continually for insight into all situations and circumstances
124. Aim to learn more, than to be right

125. Respect time of others-it is a precious commodity
126. Do not be afraid
127. Remember everyone will not be kind, be an example
128. Take a stand-do not run away from a challenge
129. Remember that I have significance
130. Remember God has a plan for my life
131. Seek guidance from those who have more experience
132. Pace myself to accomplish daily goals
133. Stay in contact with family, friends and those who inspire me
134. We all have a dash between the day we are born and the day we die
135. Make your dash count for something positive/ make a difference
136. Never stop learning
137. Always use my creativity to enjoy life and cope with stressors
138. Remember to always teach someone what you know
139. Remember to learn from others so our culture will never be extinct
140. Don't be afraid or angry of not getting the credit for anything
141. God knows all and sees what we do to build up the Kingdom
142. Learn not to forget myself in all my giving. Save a small portion for me
143. Compassion for others can go a long way
144. Remember everyone is dealing with something even if it is "denial"
145. Keep my environment clean
146. It's ok to cry, it demonstrates sensitivity and the road towards healing
147. Do not hesitate to share what you know. You will not become obsolete
148. Be ready to "Pass the baton" so you can be promoted and grow.
149. Passing the Baton allows the next generation to put their spin on things
150. Always be ready to impart new knowledge to others

151. Be an inspiration to all people you come in contact with daily
152. Strive to make this a better world, by making yourself a better person
153. Change starts with YOU.
154. Learn to take breaks and not feel guilty about it
155. Refuel your mind, body and spirit- it can be your lifeline to new potential
156. Embrace those who have your best interest at heart
157. Pray for those who are your "haters" and wish you no Good Will
158. Always look up —no matter what the circumstances-stay optimistic
159. Seek more to understand, than to be understood
160. Consult with the manufacturer of my life God-when making life changes
161. Make Plans, with room for change from God – He knows what is best
162. Stay fiscally strong, invest and understand the purpose for money
163. Make a habit of saving for a rainy day
164. Set boundaries with others, it helps with preventing blurred lines
165. Do not allow myself to be manipulated by others
166. Keep my goals close to the vest and share on an as needed basis
167. Practice physical distance to avoid contracting COVID-19, negative energy
168. Honor those who lived before us. Never forget their accomplishments
169. Continue the cause for social justice, civil rights, equity and
170. Embrace and practice inclusion of individual differences
171. Turn off the TV for a while and spend time with myself
172. Limit my news watching
173. Expect and look for blessings big and small

174. Learn to Breathe (faith, hope, love, charity and change)
175. Trust my gut instinct
176. Learn to be proactive and less reactive
177. Always continue learning, both formally and informally
178. Always encourage others to aspire to greatness
179. In the big scheme of things, we all win! In the end
180. Embrace change, expect change and adapt and be flexible to change
181. Read the book "Who Moved My Cheese?" It illustrates change well.
182. I see myself as all of those characters from the book from time to time.
183. Remember you are significant and your contributions matter
184. Hone your craft often, be ready to be used by God at any minute
185. Practice, Practice, Practice. Perfect your skills so that it becomes natural
186. Appreciate the greatness in others whatever the area of expertise
187. I believe God made us different so that we would depend on each other
188. Be ready to "switch gears" at any moment.
189. Submission is an act of reverence
190. Recognize the needs of others, your community and be a blessing
191. Recognize the importance of taking care of ourselves
192. Find time to pray
193. Find your niche in life
194. It's all about perspective
195. Learn to reframe everything —don't take everything personally
196. Have fun, learn to smile- it makes for a more pleasant day for everyone
197. Embrace solitude-learn to love myself
198. Look inward for self-worth

199. Look inward for self-esteem
200. Look upward for promotion
201. Look outward for joining with others
202. Look outward for assessing how to adjust
203. Look onward for hope/change
204. Remember God orders our steps

Sunday August 16, 2020

Thank you Lord for my life. Today was a sad morning receiving news of the death of two extended family members. One was a surprise, the other one I had some preparation. Remembering that control lies with God gives me solace and peace. Lord please continue to direct my path.

In all thy ways acknowledge him, and he shall direct thy paths. Be not wise in thine own eyes: fear the LORD, and depart from evil.

-Proverbs 3:6-7 King James Version

PART III

CELEBRATION

Enjoying and celebrating our relationships are vital. Included are preselected images of family, friends and loved ones who have uplifted me, embraced me and fueled me to become the person I am today. Enjoy

The Big Day!! I feel the excitement. Beautiful!

7

Beautiful Couple!
Wishing you both the best Leah and Nick.

Dear Friends,

Faithful Friends –Carla and Andrea

Catching some sun!

Destin, FL

God makes everythingbeautiful in its time.
Ecclesiastes 3:11 ESV

All grown up and ready to see what the world
has to offer. We love you Leslie!

Gifts Galore....

Did somebody say party over here? Go Girl.

Christmas 2020! Remembering the Reason for the Season.

Christmas 2020! We almost cancelled Christmas!
(A Holiday like no other).

EASTER *Blessings*

Matriarch of the family- Momma Dot!
Enjoying the beauty of nature and celebrating every moment.

Mother and Daughter Moment

Proud DAD

Blast from the past
Rock…. Skate… Roll… Bounce …
It is never too late. Thank you George.

A new beginning!

Congratulations!!! We are proud of you both.

Newlyweds are enjoying a slice of cake. Yummy!!

The Jones Family enjoying life together.

**Mr. & Mrs. Dungee better known as
(Momma Ginny and Daddy Joe)**
Thank you for your excellence and service. We love you!
We strive to make you proud.

We love you and miss you Ronnie and Peggy-
Your family and God Children! (Adrian & Reggie)

A Daddy Daughter Moment-
(Reggie and Mady)

Flying high! The sky is the limit!!
Go Reggie and Mady

MeMa and Mady!

Aunt Emma – Eufaula, AL We Love you Auntie!

Andrea & Aunt Mary – Eufaula, AL We love you Auntie.

Man's best friend! Owner, Virgil and pet Kudjoe

Aunt "Birdie-Bernice" to us and "B.B. King" to others
You are still our inspiration and in our hearts. You
helped us get our start in life. We thank you!

and her Beautiful, Stylish, Sassy, & Intelligent daughter & our Cuz Debra.....May they both Rest In Peace♥.

PART IV

CORPORATION

MOVING ONTO HIGHER GROUND, INC. (NON PROFIT) PDF INSERT

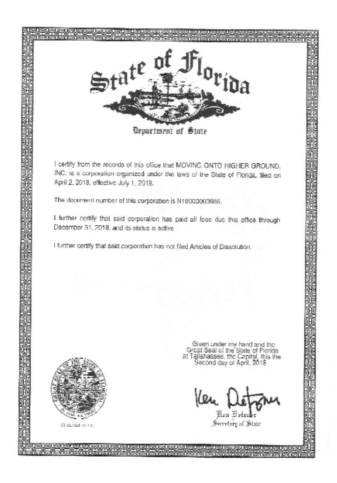

State of Florida

Department of State

I certify from the records of this office that MOVING ONTO HIGHER GROUND, INC. is a corporation organized under the laws of the State of Florida, filed on April 2, 2018, effective July 1, 2018.

The document number of this corporation is N18000003666.

I further certify that said corporation has paid all fees due this office through December 31, 2018, and its status is active.

I further certify that said corporation has not filed Articles of Dissolution.

Given under my hand and the Great Seal of the State of Florida at Tallahassee, the Capital, this the Second day of April, 2018

Ken Detzner
Secretary of State

State of Florida
Department of State

I certify from the records of this office that MOVING ONTO HIGHER GROUND, INC. is a corporation organized under the laws of the State of Florida, filed on April 2, 2018, effective July 1, 2018.

The document number of this corporation is N18000003665.

I further certify that said corporation has paid all fees due this office through December 31, 2021, that its most recent annual report/uniform business report was filed on February 12, 2021, and that its status is active.

I further certify that said corporation has not filed Articles of Dissolution.

Given under my hand and the
Great Seal of the State of Florida
at Tallahassee, the Capital, this
the Twelfth day of February, 2021

Secretary of State

Tracking Number: 5900867853CC

To authenticate this certificate, visit the following site, enter this number, and then follow the instructions displayed.

https://services.sunbiz.org/Filings/CertificateOfStatus/CertificateAuthentication

MOVING ONTO HIGHER GROUND, INC.
P.O. BOX 222365
WEST PALM BEACH, FLORIDA 33422
AndrBow5@aol.com
PHONE # (561) 801-2405

"Meeting life's challenges one step at a time"

Moving Onto Higher Ground, Inc. was established in 2005 for the sole purpose of inspiring children and families to overcome life's challenges through the use of dance and movement. Child-Centered and Family-Focused, MOHG's primary goal is to provide a constructive outlet for our children and families through the following methods:

> Educational workshops; motivational speaking engagements
> Presentations on personal growth, development and safety
> Solution-Focused Therapeutic counseling sessions incorporating the use of dance and creative movement to improve physical, mental and spiritual health
> Psychotherapy, Behavioral Assessments, Risk, Stress & Anger Management
> Resource and Referrals to community organizations
> Live dance performances for various organizations in an effort to uplift the human spirit, motivate and inspire the human soul to reach higher heights.

Based in Palm Beach County, Florida, we also provide services in Hillsborough County. The key focus of this organization is to become a catalyst for positive change in the lives of individuals within Palm Beach County and abroad. Sessions are facilitated by a Licensed Clinical Social Worker and Certified Family Life Educator.

MOHG, Inc. is a faith-based organization founded on the principles of faith, hope and love. We encourage you to explore an alternative approach to change through the connection of holistic health, incorporating mind, body and spirit.

Thank you for your interest in MOHG, Inc., where we answer to a higher calling.

Founder/President
Andrea Bowen, LCSW, CFLE

Moving Onto Higher Ground, Inc. Fiscal Report can be obtained by requesting at www.movingontohigherground.com

Contact Author: Andrea Bowen

In your email, put Fiscal Report Request in your Subject line

Thank you.

As I close this chapter of my life, I say thank you Lord for allowing me the opportunity to see this day. Today is the day I took my first dosage of the COVID-19 Vaccination. I only wish this opportunity could have been made available to the 527,917 individuals who unfortunately have transitioned earlier than intended. This book is due in memory to you.

Tree of Life!

EPILOGUE

As I close this segment of my book I am truly running a race
against time. I set a timeline and I have gone well beyond it. I
am physically exhausted as I am in transition, seeking to change
homes and secondary employment. I am totally empty, but manage
to muster up enough energy to add these final words. I have done
everything I believe I have been appointed to do in my current
circumstances. I truly believe God has more for me. I believe God
has more for you too. Our environment shapes us. As a social
worker we are taught about the significance of outside factors/
the environment on our relationships, perspective and overall
demeanor. Sometimes we may need to alter our environment,
in order to be productive and live upright for God's acceptance.
Right now I am thankful that I have had the opportunity to
write this book in the safety of my home. I am grateful to be
able to finish my story and hope that God will bless this piece of
literature. I hope and pray that this document will serve as a means
to uplift you and also give you food for thought. I humbly pray
that there will be growth and development in your life. Hoping
for the best and praying for God's Will to be done in your life.
Sometimes we don't truly know the impact our words, (both the
spoken and written) can have on an individual, group or culture
of people. This is my outlet. I have always been introspective
and find pleasure and joy in sharing my dreams, goals and
things I love. I am praying that you find your niche in life and

that you embrace it. Figure out what you love and do it because someone may just be waiting for you to be an answer for them, a word of comfort for them, a spirit of encouragement or living example of what is good in the world. Most importantly, Live Life Abundantly and show love to each other in word and deed.

Keep the Faith! & Fight the Good Fight!

Striving to leave a legacy of love, compassion, and creativity

Andrea
March 24, 2021
8:00 PM

Suggested Readings
and Cites

Bronner, Dale C Bishop/ Dr. ***Pass the Baton: The Miracle of Mentoring***. Carnegie Books 212 Riverside Parkway Austelle, GA 30168 2006.

Bowen, Andrea. ***Time Out: Practicing Self-Care*** Xlibris, LLC 2014.

Bowen, Andrea. ***H3: Harmonious, Healthy & Heaven-Sent Union*** Xlibris, LLC 2015.

Carlson, Kristine. ***Don't sweat the small stuff for women: Simple and practical ways to do what matters most and find time for you.*** Hyperion Hallmark Cards: New York: 2001.

Chapman, Gary Dr. ***The 5 love languages: The secret to love that lasts.*** Northfield Publishing: Chicago, IL 2015.

Holy Bible, New International Version, NIV Copyright 1973, 1978, 1984, 2011 by Biblica, Inc.

Spencer, Johnson M.D. ***Who moved my cheese?*** G.P. Putnam's Sons. New York, NY 1998.

Stanford, David. ***Holy Bible-King James Version***. *Oxford University Press, London.*

Whitaker, Angela G. Rev./ Dr. ***Rolling in Greatness***. Peacemakers, Inc. Tallahassee, FL 2004.

PART V

COMPILATION

H3

HARMONIOUS, HEALTHY & HEAVEN-SENT UNION

Andrea Bowen

This book serves to provide practical and spiritual guidance to couples preparing to unite and become one in holy matrimony. This book focuses on providing tips and strategies to preparing for life transition, cultivating healthy relationships. The intent of this project is to help others in finding ways to deal with time management and stress management as it relates to planning your special wedding and most importantly examining ways to sustain a healthy marriage and cultivating a positive and loving relationship with the love of your life.

Hardback 978-1-5144-2330-1 | $24.99
Paperback 978-1-5144-2329-5 | $15.99
E-book 978-1-5144-2328-8 | $3.99

Available now from

Xlibris

www.xlibris.com

H3: Harmonious, Healthy &
Heaven –Sent Union
Text Published by Xlibris
(Total of 65 pages including front and back cover)

Time Out
Practicing Self Care

A N D R E A   B O W E N

Time Out focuses on providing an inspirational approach to developing self-worth, strengthening coping skills, and finding alternative perspectives to life's challenges. The book is designed to help individuals find ways to examine the importance of slowing down and taking time to stop what we are doing from our regular ordinary lifestyle in order to gain momentum and a fresh look at the future.

The book aims at helping one gain the right perspective for their life through looking at multiple life lessons as seen through the eyes of the author, Busy-Bee-Tina. The book provides visual examples of the author's year of taking time out at various locations and how she learns to regroup and move forward in her personal and professional endeavors.

ISBN13 Softcover : 978-1-4990-8272-2
ISBN13 Hardcover : 978-1-4990-8271-5
ISBN13 eBook : 978-1-4990-8273-9

Published by Xlibris
Order Today!
Call +1-888-795-4274
or order online at
www.xlibris.com,
www.amazon.com,
www.barnesandnoble.com,
or visit your local bookstore.

WRITE YOUR OWN SUCCESS

Time Out: Practicing Self Care
Text Published by Xlibris
(Total of 85 pages including front and back cover)